W9-APO-882

FLOWERS FROM SEED TO BLOOM

By George Pendergast

Gareth Stevens
PUBLISHING

Please visit our website, www.garethstevens.com. For a free color catalog of all our high-quality books, call toll free 1-800-542-2595 or fax 1-877-542-2596.

Library of Congress Cataloging-in-Publication Data

Pendergast, George, author.
Flowers : from seeds to bloom / George Pendergast.
    pages cm. — (Cycles in nature)
Includes bibliographical references and index.
ISBN 978-1-4824-1659-6 (pbk.)
ISBN 978-1-4824-1660-2 (6 pack)
ISBN 978-1-4824-1658-9 (library binding)
1. Flowers—Juvenile literature. 2. Flowers—Life cycles—Juvenile literature. 3. Seeds—Juvenile literature. I. Title.
QK49.P46 2015
582.13—dc23
                                    2014028203

Published in 2016 by
Gareth Stevens Publishing
111 East 14th Street, Suite 349
New York, NY 10003

Designer: Sarah Liddell
Editor: Ryan Nagelhout

Photo credits: Cover, p. 1 dookfish/Shutterstock.com; p. 5 Mizuri/Shutterstock.com; p. 7 Chepko Danil Vitalevich/Shutterstock.com; p. 9 amenic181/Shutterstock.com; p. 11 MyLoupe/UIG/Universal Images Group/Getty Images; pp. 13, 17 (plant)ChaiyonS021/Shutterstock.com; p. 15 Bildagentur Zoonar GmbH/Shutterstock.com; p. 17 (seeds) kzww/Shutterstock.com; p. 17 (soil) Tashatuvango/Shutterstock.com; p. 17 (flower) Palto/Shutterstock.com; p. 17 (plant with seeds) Timofeyev Alexander/Shutterstock.com; p. 17 (background) Pakhnyushcha/Shutterstock.com; p. 19 Bonnie Sue Rauch/Photo Researchers/Getty Images; p. 21 Biehler Michael/Shutterstock.com.

Printed in the United States of America

CPSIA compliance information: Batch #CS16GS: For further information contact Gareth Stevens, New York, New York at 1-800-542-2595.

CONTENTS

Boldface words appear in the glossary.

Growing Flowers

The life of a plant always follows the same stages. From seed to flower, plant life has a **pattern**. This is called a life **cycle**. Let's learn more about the life cycle of a flowering plant!

Starting with Seeds

Most plants come from seeds. These seeds may be very, very small, but they can grow into huge plants. The seeds have a shell, or seed coat, around them to keep everything safe inside.

Different plants have different kinds of seeds. They also need different things to grow. Most seeds need to be in soil to grow. Most need sunlight and warmth. Seeds need water to grow and start making flowers.

9

Swelling Seeds

The seed coat takes in the water, and the seed starts to swell, or grow bigger. When it has enough water, it breaks open! Plant parts start to come out of the shell. Roots start to grow down into the soil.

The roots take in water and **nutrients** to help the plant grow. The plant pushes up through the soil and aboveground. The plant uses light from the sun to make food. This is called **photosynthesis**.

Flower Power

When the plant grows big enough, it makes a flower. Part of the plant grows a bud. Then the bud opens its flower up wide. The flower is in **bloom**! The flower helps make new flowering plants.

Some flowers have many different parts. Other flowers only have certain parts needed to **reproduce**. They need help to make new flowers. Many flowers are bright and bring animals close. The animals help the flowers reproduce.

A Sunflower's Life Cycle

seed

plant grows

flower blooms

flower
makes seeds

17

Birds and Bees

Birds and bees carry pollen from some flowers to others. This is called pollination. When the flowers are pollinated, they make seeds. Some plants make fruit! This fruit has seeds inside.

Starting Over

Now the seeds have to be spread to grow new plants. Some seeds are blown by the wind. Animals move other seeds to new places, too. When the seeds reach the soil, the cycle of seed to bloom starts all over again!

GLOSSARY

bloom: the flowering state of a plant

cycle: a series of events that happen over and over again

nutrient: something a living thing needs to grow and stay alive

pattern: the way things happen over and over again

photosynthesis: the process plants use to make food with sunlight, water, and a gas called carbon dioxide

reproduce: to make new life

FOR MORE INFORMATION

BOOKS

Lawrence, Ellen. *From Bird Poop to Wind: How Seeds Get Around.* New York, NY: Bearport Publishing, 2013.

Lundgren, Julie K. and Kristi Lew. *Plant Life Cycles.* North Mankato, MN: Rourke Publishing, 2012.

Rattini, Kristin Baird. *Seed to Plant.* Washington, DC: National Geographic, 2014.

WEBSITES

Flowering Plants
www.ducksters.com/science/biology/flowering_plants.php
Learn more about what happens inside a flowering plant.

Life Cycle of a Plant
sciencekids.co.nz/gamesactivities/lifecycles.html
Label the parts of a flower in this interactive game.

INDEX

DATE DUE

			PRINTED IN U.S.A.